Ollie Visits
Where it All Started

ILLUSTRATED BY
Milt Priggee

WRITTEN BY
Lawrence Blundred

Ollie Otter Adventures Series, Book 3
Ollie Visits Where It All Started
Published by
DP Kids Press
244 5th Avenue, Suite G-200
NY, NY 10001
646-233-4366
www.DocUmeantPublishing.com

No part of this publication may be reproduced, stored in a retrieval system, or transmitted in any way by any means—electronic, mechanical, photocopy, recording, or otherwise—without the prior permission of the copyright holder, except as provided by USA copyright law.

Disclaimer: This is a work of fiction. All characters appearing in this work are fictitious. Any resemblance to real persons, living or dead, is purely coincidental.

Cover & Interior Illustrator: Milt Priggee
Editor: Philip S. Marks

Cover Design & Layout: Ginger Marks
DocUmeant Designs
www.DocUmeantDesigns.com

ISBN: 9781950075058 (pbk)
ISBN: 9781957832081 (epub)

Library of Congress Cataloging-in-Publication Data

Names: Blundred, Lawrence, author. | Priggee, Milt, 1953- illustrator.
Title: Ollie visits where it all started / written by Lawrence Blundred ; illustrated by Milt Priggee.
Description: Book 3 commemorative edition. | NY, NY : DP Kids Press, [2023] | Series: Ollie Otter adventures series ; 3 | Audience: Ages 6-12 | Audience: Grades 4-6 | Summary: Ollie Otter and best friend Bonnie Bunny travel to Bainbridge Island where pickleball was first played, and along the way he makes new friends and meets a long-lost relative.
Identifiers: LCCN 2023030854 (print) | LCCN 2023030855 (ebook) | ISBN 9781950075058 (paperback) | ISBN 9781957832081 (epub)
Subjects: CYAC: Otters--Fiction. | Pickleball (Game)--Fiction. | Racket games--Fiction. | Friendship--Fiction. | Bainbridge Island (Wash.)--Fiction. | LCGFT: Picture books.
Classification: LCC PZ7.1.B643 Ol 2023 (print) | LCC PZ7.1.B643 (ebook) | DDC [E]--dc23
LC record available at https://lccn.loc.gov/2023030854
LC ebook record available at https://lccn.loc.gov/2023030855

Ollie Visits Where It All Started is dedicated to the truth that families matter. Yes, often families can be 'messy'. We are not all born into the same type of family. Some families are small; some large. Some families grow with time; others do not. Some of us are born into a family with a mom and dad. Others are welcomed into a new family with adopted parents or grandparents. Sometimes families are formed when friends meet new friends and they share great adventures together! Families may not look alike, but they all have the potential to provide love and a sense of belonging.

Ollie Visits Where It All Started is dedicated to the truth that families matter. Yes, often families can be 'messy'. We are not all born into the same type of family. Some families are small; some large. Some families grow with time; others do not. Some of us are born into a family with a mom and dad. Others are welcomed into a new family with adopted parents or grandparents. Sometimes families are formed when friends meet new friends and they share great adventures together! Families may not look alike, but they all have the potential to provide love and a sense of belonging.

Foreword

Larry and I met through the wonderful world of pickleball. He has a contagious enthusiasm for sharing the sport we all love thru his writings and the characters in his children's books where he extends a hand to readers of all ages, sizes, and shapes.

Larry and I both have a deep desire to give back to the sport and the people we have met along the way—paying it forward again and again. Cultivating the next generation of "pickleballers," and especially those with some form of special, unique challenge—young or old—hold a special place in Larry's heart.

Pickleball is so much more than just a sport. The health benefits, friendships, and connections made are priceless—just like what you will find in Larry's books with the characters (he calls them "critters") he weaves into positive stories of family, community, love, and encouragement.

Everyone in the world needs pickleball and Larry and I are just a few of the many that continue to spread the FUN and lasting love of this amazing sport. Larry has chosen a unique way of conveying this love through stories featuring his lead "critter" Ollie Otter and so many others who bring smiles, chuckles and, yes, perhaps a few tears (the good ones!).

I welcome, and thank, Larry for the opportunity to introduce you to *Ollie Visits Where It All Started*. **Get ready for more fun, smiles, family connections**—all taking place where pickleball did indeed start, Bainbridge Island, and where Larry's new critters travel, connect and, of course, head to the Founder's Tournament!

Jennifer Lucore

Jennifer is a professional pickleball player, global ambassador, inductee into the Pickleball Hall of Fame, USA Pickleball historian AND coauthored, with her mom, the sport's first-ever history book: *The History of Pickleball – More Than 50 Years of Fun!* **Her numerous gold medal championships include 17-time USA Pickleball Nationals, 11-time Canadian Nationals, 6-time Huntsman World Senior Games, 6-time International Tournaments, 4-time Tournament of Champions, and many golds at the US Open and pro tours. She is also known to have her sidekick, doubles partner, Alex Hamner around her, for together they have achieved 5 USA Pickleball Open/Pro Doubles National Championships (2011–2014, 2016).**

Introduction

In my first book, How Pickleball Saved Ollie Otter, Ollie was adopted. With the help of Mr. and Mrs. Pickleball, Ollie was introduced to a new family that took him in, loved him, and introduced him to pickleball. Ollie had new parents and a new community of pickleball players and friends. Ollie, Robby Racoon, Pauly Penguin, and Wally Wallaby—each with special and unique families—discovered the game of pickleball. And each critter found love, strength, support, and acceptance as they were introduced to this amazing sport.

After the four critters met at a tournament in Cincinnati, Ohio, they each returned home with a dream and vision to spread their love of pickleball to other critters, some of whom (they discovered) had unique abilities and challenges. The animal friends in Ollie and His Pickleball Friends Return Home remind us that pickleball can be for everyone and every family!

When the founders of pickleball created the sport in 1965, three distinct families came together to solve what was then a problem and a challenge: their children were complaining that there was not enough to do. The kids were bored. They did not have video games to play. How many puzzles or games of checkers or Monopoly could be played without tiring of them? The kids played outside for the most part, but they did not have tennis or basketball courts on every corner! To intensify the problem, these families lived on an Island, where there were likely as many vacationers as residents.

What the families did have was a driveway, a badminton net, and some paddles. Maybe someone had a whiffle ball and a bat. Apparently, they did, because the first pickleball was a whiffle ball. There was a hard surface too—the driveway! With thoughts of tennis and badminton in mind, the three families created the first pickleball court. The driveway already had lines for playing badminton, so they did not need to paint lines for a pickleball court. They just used the lines that were there, which is why pickleball has the same size court as badminton, give or take a few inches for the kitchen line!

There were other problems to solve: whiffle balls cracked easily and the paddles were too small. This book is not where you will find the rest of the story of how pickleball developed. You can find that in a book titled *History of Pickleball: More Than 50 Years of Fun!* by Jennifer Lucore and Beverly Youngren. I highly recommend you get this book, as it covers the first 52 years of the sport. (Jennifer hopes to release an updated version in 2023.) What matters here is that three families came together to solve a problem—and they created something that was and is fun, was and is challenging, was and is something that brings people and families together to this day!

The game these families created in a driveway is now the fastest growing sport in the USA and, by some counts, the world. I am doubtful that Barney McCallum, Joel Pritchard, or Bill Bell—and their children and families—had any idea what would become of the game they created in 1965—at that time a game which did not even have a name! The name came later: pickleball. When asked about the history of the name, Barney always said, "Pickleball was named after the family dog, Pickles." That dog had a sister named LuLu. So, the game could have been called "Luluball"! Don't you agree: "Pickleball" sounds better?

Keep smiling with pickleball and enjoy this newest release from Ollie Otter Books and Ollie Otter Enterprises.

"Well, Bonnie, we are on our way," Ollie said as he looked over the ship's side rail.

He watched and listened to the gentle waves of Puget Sound. *Splish*. *Splash*. His best friend, Bonnie Bunny, stood beside him.

"For a minute, I didn't think we would make it on the ferry," Bonnie replied. "They allow dogs, of course, but we were the first otter and bunny traveling together." Bonnie smiled.

"I was worried too," Ollie said. "I think it helped when we told the ticket man why we were going to Bainbridge Island. We want to learn more about where the game of pickleball started."

"Yes! That helped," Bonnie giggled. "The ticket man said he loves to play pickleball . . . and he said otters are one of his favorite critters!"

"I am sure he likes bunnies, too," Ollie smiled. "Everyone loves bunnies!" Bonny nodded and smiled shyly.

Ollie reached into his bag to get a snack. "Bonnie, I am a little hungry. Would you like a snack? I eat fish and frogs when I am at home, but for the trip I brought fish-shaped gummies and fish-shaped cheese crackers." Ollie gave one of each to Bonnie.

"Thank you, Ollie," said Bonnie. "Yum, these are good. Would you like some of my snacks? I brought carrots, of course, but I also brought red chewy licorice sticks. Want some?"

"I'll take a chewy licorice stick, but I'll pass on the carrots," Ollie said with a grin. "Thank you."

As Ollie put the gummies and crackers back in his bag, he spotted an envelope and pulled it out.

"Bonnie, I think someone put an envelope in my bag. It says: 'To Ollie and Bonnie' on the outside."

Ollie opened the envelope and saw a letter. It was from Mr. and Mrs. Pickleball.

"Please read the letter, Ollie," Bonnie said.

Ollie started reading:

Dear Ollie and Bonnie,

We are happy for you. You are taking a big trip to a special place. Take time to meet new critters and people. Listen and learn. Make new friends. Explore and have fun! Be safe.

We love you!
Mr. and Mrs. Pickleball

P.S. Because you are going to the Northwest in the United States, I want to tell you something. Years ago, before your mother died, she told me that she had a sister who had moved to one of the states in the Northwest. You never know who you might meet!

"Wow, that letter is special," Ollie said. "They must have tucked it into my backpack at the airport. They knew I would find it."

"And you did, Ollie! That makes me happy."
Bonnie hopped up and down again.

The two friends looked up and saw Bainbridge Island at the same time. "Bonnie, look! We are almost there!" shouted Ollie.

"It is so beautiful," Bonnie said quietly. "Look at those Monterey Pine and Douglas Fir trees! They are so tall and strong."

"Yes, Bonnie, they are! Did you know that one tree on the island is over 150 feet tall?"

"How do you know that?" Bonnie asked.

"Well," Ollie said, "I read a book about the island. It's a very special island. It is where pickleball started, but there is so much more."

"And we get to explore and discover it together!" Bonnie couldn't stop hopping.

Soon Bonnie and Ollie were skipping off the ferry. People welcomed them with friendly smiles.

"Can I help you?" one man asked.

"Well," Ollie said. "We just arrived. We want to get some ice cream, look at the island map, and plan our trip."

"You can't go wrong with any of the ice cream shops on the Island," the man said. "Some of my favorites are just minutes from here. Turn left at Winslow street and enjoy!"

"Thank you, Sir," Bonnie said. "Ollie, let's get a cone from each place and plan our trip!"

So, they hopped and waddled along their way to get ice cream. Map in hand!

Licking their ice cream cones, Ollie and Bonnie walked up Winslow Way and spotted a bookstore.

"Bonnie, this looks like a neat place! 'Eagle Harbor Book Co.' Let's go in and look around."

"Wow," Bonnie said. "They have all kinds of things, not just books. Look, here is a table that has books about local critters. And ... a book about the history of pickleball!"

"Bonnie, I think we should buy that book right now." Ollie opened the book. "Hmm, it's written by Jennifer Lucore and her mother, Beverly Youngren."

Ollie turned the page. "Look at that, Bonnie! A picture of the authors with one of the people who started pickleball here on the island, Mr. Barney McCallum! I think this book will help us as we travel."

"What is our next stop, Ollie?" Bonnie asked.

Ollie looked at the map. "We are close to the Bainbridge Island Historical Museum. The museum might have interesting stuff and people who can help us plan our trip."

'That is a great idea, Ollie. Let's turn up this street, Ericksen Avenue. The museum is on the left," said Bonnie. "Let's go inside."

"Hello," Ollie said to the museum guide. "I am Ollie, and this is Bonnie. We came to the island to meet new critters, make new friends, explore, and learn about where pickleball started."

"Welcome to the museum," Charlie the attendant said. "We are happy to have visitors. Let me walk you around."

Ollie and Bonnie followed the guide to a room that had all kinds of exhibits. The first area they entered was an exhibit about pickleball.

"Look, Bonnie," said Ollie. "There's a picture of the three men who started pickleball—Barney, Joel Pritchard, and Bill Bell."

Bonnie pointed to a special case. "Look at that, Ollie. A really old paddle made of wood! It was made in 1968—the first paddle sold in stores!"

"Wow, that is awesome!" Ollie was excited. "The paddles we use at home are fancier, but I am sure this old paddle did the job!"

Ollie and Bonnie toured the rest of the museum.

"I think we are ready to go, Bonnie," Ollie said.

Bonnie nodded. "The nice people at the bookstore and the museum guide helped us so much. And we have our map. Let's go!" Bonnie bounced down the steps.

"Wait for me!" Ollie laughed. "First, we will go to Strawberry Park. What a yummy name for a park!"

Soon the two friends were at the park, and yes, there were strawberries growing wild. "I think we are allowed to pick a few. I am hungry again!" Ollie rubbed his belly.

"I love strawberries!" Bonnie said as she nibbled on a berry. Then she pointed to something. "Look, over there. It's a dog park! See that cute dog? Let's go meet him—or her."

Ollie walked over and stretched out a paw. "Hi, my name is Ollie, and this is my friend Bonnie. What is your name?"

"My name is Dilly," the doggie said.

"I like your name. It is different," Ollie said. "How did you get that name?"

"My grandpa's name was Pickles. My parents wanted to give me a name that honored Grandpa Pickles."

Ollie smiled. "I get it ... Dilly Pickles—like Dill Pickles!"

"Yes, you got it!" Dilly laughed.

"Now wait a minute! That name... Pickles. Pickles... as in pickleball?" Ollie asked.

"Yes, you got that right too," Dilly said. "Pickleball was named after my Grandpa Pickles."

"How did that happen, Dilly?" Bonnie was curious.

"Well," Dilly said proudly, "as the story goes, my grandfather would always chase the ball when people were playing. So, when the families, who invented the game, were choosing a name for their new sport, they called it 'pickleball.'"

"That is sure is a fun fact!" Bonnie said.

"I was told that my grandfather had a sister. Her name was LuLu. I guess if she had chased the loose balls more than Grandpa Pickles, the game might have been called 'Luluball.'"

They all laughed. Then Ollie had an idea. "Dilly, can you join us on our trip? Our next stop is the Grand Forest."

"I would love to join you," Dilly said. "I can help you get there. Just let me tell my parents that I am helping some new friends.

They will be happy that I want to do that!"

Soon the three critters were off to the Grand Forest, with Dilly leading the way. They trotted and waddled and hopped through the towering dense trees and pines.

They listened to birds warble and tweet and caw. They looked at colorful fields of pink and purple and red dahlias. And they met more new friends—Daisy Dear and her brother Digger Deer!

Daisy and Digger joined the critter adventure. It was like a fun animal parade! When they got to Frog Rock and Frog Hollow, they had a group picture taken.

Looking at the map, Ollie said, "Let's head to Point No Point Park!" Ollie was excited to go there because he had heard that other otters were living there.

Along the way, the lively group of friends heard a familiar sound: Dink! Donk! Pop! Pickleball courts were everywhere on the island, including the Founders Courts at Battle Point Park. The sound made Ollie and Bonnie smile. That was the same sound they heard back home.

"I love that sound," Ollie said. "I remember the first time I heard it. I was alone then, but now I have a family—and lots of friends!"

"We'll visit the pickleball courts later and make more friends," Bonnie said.

"We sure will!" Ollie exclaimed excitedly.

When the critters arrived at Point No Point Park, they saw a lighthouse. Part of the roof was red. The windows were neatly trimmed in black. Climbing the front porch steps, the critters saw a sign on the door: "CLOSED TO VISITORS." They all moaned.

"Let's just knock on the door anyway and see what happens," Dilly Dog said.

"Good idea," Bonnie said. So, they knocked and knocked, but no one came to open the door.

"Oh, well," sighed Ollie. "Let's just walk to the beach. It is so pretty there."

As they turned to go, they heard the door open . . . just a tiny bit. A squeaky little voice said, "Whoa! Wait a minute! Can I help you?"

Surprised, the critters looked around. Where had the voice come from? They didn't see anyone standing at the door. Then Digger the Deer looked down. He spotted a small mouse wearing a visor, spectacles, and a striped shirt. The mouse was holding a tiny broom in his paw.

"Hello," continued the perky voice. "I am Louis the Lighthouse Mouse. I help keep the lighthouse tidy." Louis jumped up on the porch rail to make himself taller.

Ollie lowered his head until he was eye-to-eye with the little mouse. "Hi, Louis. I am Ollie," he said. "These are my friends. We heard there are otters at this park, and we want to meet them and make new friends."

"You came to the right place," Louis said. "See the marsh behind the lighthouse? Lots of otter families live there." Louis pointed to a big drainpipe. "Sometimes, you can see the otters sliding down this pipe that runs from the marsh down to the beach. It looks so fun!"

Just then, Ollie and his friends saw a young otter jump into the open end of the pipe. "Look out below. Here I come!" he yelled. "*Whee!*"

The otter went spinning down the pipe until he tumbled out onto the beach at the other end. The critters laughed and ran to meet the young otter.

"Hello," said Ollie. "What is your name?"

"I am Oscar," the young otter said proudly.

"I like that name," Ollie said. "Oscar, these are my friends—Bonnie, Dilly, Daisy Deer, and her brother Digger. And this is Louis the Lighthouse Mouse. He said we might find some otters sliding through the pipe—and he was right!"

"It is so fun, Ollie! Want to join me? Have you ever slid down a drainpipe? Do you and your friends live on Bainbridge Island? Oscar was full of questions.

Ollie laughed. "Dilly, Daisy, and Digger live on the island, but Bonnie and I are from the state of Michigan. We are here to explore, make new friends, and learn about where pickleball started.

Oscar thought for a moment. "Before I was born, my mom and dad lived in Michigan. They came to visit the Northwest and decided to stay. We love it here!"

Ollie started to get excited. "Oscar, you and I have Michigan in common, because of our parents."

Then Ollie looked at Bonnie. "Bonnie, do you remember the last words in the note from Mr. and Mrs. Pickleball? They said my mom had a sister who had moved to this part of the country—the Northwest."

"Yes. I remember," Bonnie nodded with enthusiasm.

Ollie looked back at Oscar. "Oscar, did your mother ever say if she had a sister back in Michigan?"

"Yes," Oscar replied. "Mama said her sister died at an early age. But before she died, she had an otter pup—a boy."

"Do you know the name of your mother's sister?" Ollie asked.

"Olive . . . No, that's not right. Olivia," Oscar said, matter-of-factly.

Ollie's eyes opened wide: "Oscar, my mother's name was Olivia!" Oscar and Ollie stared at each other. They grinned. Their mothers had been sisters, so . . .

"We're cousins!" the two otters shouted together. Then they gave each other a big high-five!

"We have to go back to the marsh and tell Mama!" Oscar took off, leading the way to the marsh, with Ollie and the other critters following close behind.

"Mama! Mama!" Oscar shouted. "I have big news. This is my cousin. He is from Michigan. His mother was your sister Olivia."

"Whoa, slow down," said Mama. "What is your new friend's name? Wait . . . let me guess . . . Ollie? That's the name my sister wrote on the back of this baby picture she sent to me years ago."

Mama Otter pulled a picture from her pocket and handed it to Ollie. He looked at the picture of the baby otter and turned the picture over slowly. Tears came to his eyes. There was his name, carefully printed on the back of the picture: OLLIE. Mama Otter and Oscar hugged Ollie.

"Come on, everybody! Let's go back to the beach!" shouted Oscar. "We are going to celebrate this special family reunion with a splash party!"

And that's just what they did!

Oscar's mother had prepared special snacks for all the critters.

Looking over at Oscar Ollie asked, "Have you signed up for the Founder's Tournament yet?"

"No, we need to do that! I hope there's still time."

"I am sure there is," Daisy said. "Digger and I have entered the doubles play."

"So have we!" Dilly exclaimed, smiling at Oscar.

As they sat on the beach munching on their treats, Mama cleared her throat and asked everyone to be quiet. She looked directly at Ollie and said, "Ollie, you and Bonnie can stay with us as long as you like. You are family."

Then, looking at all the critters, Mama said with a wink, "Families matter. No matter how far apart we may be, love and memories can bring us together."

(To be continued!)

BAINBRIDGE ISLAND AND OTTER BONUS BITS

Questions
1. Are Frog Rock and Frog Hollow real places?
2. What flower do you see all throughout the island?
3. What park is named after a delicious fruit?
4. What sport was founded there, and then became the official sport of the state of Washington?

Now, let's see what you know about otters.
5. Did you know there are two types of otters? Can Youi name them?
6. Do all otters sleep the same way?
7. Do all otters swim the same?

Bainbridge facts for you history buffs . . .
- For thousands of years, members of the Suquamish people and their ancestors lived on the land now called Bainbridge Island.

- There were nine villages on the island; this included winter villages at Port Madison, Battle Point, Point White, Lynwood Center, Port Blakely, and Eagle Harbor, as well as summer villages at Manzanita, Fletcher Bay, and Rolling Bay.

- In 1792, English explorer Captain George Vancouver spent several days with his ship HMS Discovery anchored off Restoration Point at the southern end of Bainbridge Island while boat parties surveyed other parts of Puget Sound.

- Vancouver spent a day exploring Rich Passage, Port Orchard, and Sinclair Inlet. He failed to find Agate Passage, and so his maps show Bainbridge Island as a peninsula, not an island.
- In 1841, US Navy Lieutenant Charles Wilkes visited the island while surveying the Pacific Northwest. Lt. Wilkes named the island after Commodore William Bainbridge, commander of the frigate USS Constitution in the War of 1812.

Want to learn more about this beautiful and historic island?
Visit the Bainbridge Island Historical Museum
https://bainbridgehistory.org/

Answer Key

1. Yes. There really is a big rock called Frog Rock, and a place called Frog Hallow on Bainbridge Island!

2. The Dahlia

3. Strawberry Park

4. Pickleball

5. Two. River Otters and Sea Otters. Guess which type of otter Ollie is? A River Otter. Remember Ollie is from Traverse City, Michigan—a long way from any sea!

6. No. Some sleep with their feet and paws entwined with other otters so they can stay together, even when sleeping.

7. No. River Otters swim on their bellies and sea otters have the lovable habit of floating on their backs. River otters swim using their four webbed feet. Sea otters use their two webbed hind feet and tail to swim.

MEET THE AUTHOR

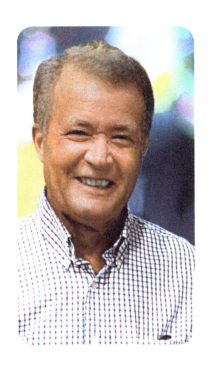

Lawrence (Larry) Blundred is a retired financial advisor. Prior to that, he served as marketing/sales director for Skyline Chili and JTM Food Group. He resides in Cincinnati, Ohio. Larry is the author of two other children's books, *How Pickleball Saved Ollie Otter* and *Ollie and His Friends Return Home*.

He and his former wife Donna, who died of a brain tumor, previously co-authored two inspirational books, *Rise Above: Survivor or Thriver?* and *Staying Resilient When Life Throws You More Than A Curveball*.

Larry and his new wife, Margo, traveled to Bainbridge Island to personally gain background for this book. He and his illustrator played football (one year!) at York High School (Elmhurst, IL) and reconnected in 2022 at their high school reunion.

MEET THE ILLUSTRATOR

Milt Priggee is an international award-winning editorial cartoonist who started his graphic commentary career with the *Chicago Daily News* in 1976. He was awarded a Journalism Fellowship to the University of Michigan from September 2000 to May 2001.

Milt has drawn editorial cartoons, caricatures, and a comic strip along with illustrations for many newspapers, magazines, books, TV specials, WEB sites and syndicates. His political cartoons have been reprinted in *Time, Newsweek, U.S. News & World Report, New York Times, Washington Post, USA Today, CNN Headline News* and *MSNBC*.

Currently, his interests are painting in oil and acrylic along with exploring the world of children's books. Milt lives with his wife Jan, also a fine artist, on Whidbey Island in the Puget Sound and are parents to four and grandparents to six.

Printed in the USA
CPSIA information can be obtained
at www.ICGtesting.com
LVHW070723220823
755931LV00016B/317